P9-CSA-666

THE
THIRTEENTH
AMENDMENT
AND ITS LEGACY

BY DUCHESS HARRIS, JD, PHD
WITH SAMANTHA S. BELL

Core Library

An Imprint of Abdo Publishing
abdobooks.com

Cover image: The Thirteenth Amendment was passed
on January 31, 1865.

abdocorelibrary.com

Published by Abdo Publishing, a division of ABDO, PO Box 398166, Minneapolis, Minnesota 55439. Copyright © 2020 by Abdo Consulting Group, Inc. International copyrights reserved in all countries. No part of this book may be reproduced in any form without written permission from the publisher. Core Library™ is a trademark and logo of Abdo Publishing.

Printed in the United States of America, North Mankato, Minnesota
022019
092019

Cover Photo: North Wind Picture Archives
Interior Photos: North Wind Picture Archives, 1, 5, 43; Shutterstock Images, 6–7; Red Line Editorial, 10, 39; Everett Historical/Shutterstock Images, 12, 17; Elaine Thompson/AP Images, 14–15; Kean Collection/Archive Photos/Getty Images, 19; National Park Service, 20; Encyclopedia Britannica/UIG Universal Images Group/Newscom, 22–23; Anton Ivanov/Shutterstock Images, 27; Universal History Archive/Universal Images Group/Getty Images, 30–31; White House Photo/Alamy, 36–37

Editor: Maddie Spalding
Series Designer: Claire Vanden Branden

Library of Congress Control Number: 2018965963

Publisher's Cataloging-in-Publication Data

Names: Harris, Duchess, author | Bell, Samantha S., author.
Title: The thirteenth amendment and its legacy / by Duchess Harris and Samantha S. Bell
Description: Minneapolis, Minnesota : Abdo Publishing, 2020 | Series: Freedom's promise | Includes online resources and index.
Identifiers: ISBN 9781532118791 (lib. bdg.) | ISBN 9781532172977 (ebook)
Subjects: LCSH: United States. Constitution. 13th Amendment--Juvenile literature. | Slavery--Law and legislation--Juvenile literature. | Slaves--Emancipation--United States--Juvenile literature. | Abolition of slavery--Juvenile literature. | Constitutional amendments--United States--Juvenile literature.
Classification: DDC 325.260973--dc23

CONTENTS

A LETTER FROM DUCHESS

The Thirteenth Amendment is one of the most important acts in the legal history of the United States. It is often said that the amendment abolished slavery. But its legacy is more complicated than that. The Thirteenth Amendment outlawed slavery except as a form of punishment. Southerners seized on this loophole. They unjustly arrested thousands of Black people. Black convicts were forced to do hard, unpaid labor. In this way, slavery was reconstructed in the South.

Freedom is a fascinating concept. Today Black people are incarcerated at more than five times the rate of white people. Are they then truly free? Who profits from the inmates' unpaid or underpaid labor? This book aims to answer these questions. It explains the events that led to the passage of the Thirteenth Amendment. It also explores how the amendment's loophole led to the mass incarceration of African Americans today.

Please join me in learning about the Thirteenth Amendment and its legacy. Follow me on a journey that examines the idea of freedom.

Duchess Harris

African Americans celebrated the passing of the Thirteenth Amendment in 1865.

A NATION DIVIDED

On June 15, 1864, 159 members of the US House of Representatives were gathered in Washington, DC. It was a hot summer day. Representatives waved fans to cool themselves. They had been debating for hours. The issue at hand was a constitutional amendment. An amendment is a change or an addition to the US Constitution. If this amendment passed, it would outlaw slavery in the United States.

The House of Representatives and the Senate both have to vote on an amendment. The House and the Senate make up the US Congress. The Senate had already voted in

US representatives meet in the US Capitol building in Washington, DC.

SLAVERY IN THE CONSTITUTION

The number of representatives a state has in the House of Representatives depends on its population. In 1787 the three-fifths clause was created. It said that an enslaved person would count as three-fifths of a person. This clause gave states that had large enslaved populations more representatives. But enslaved people could not participate in government themselves. Another slavery clause in the Constitution was called the fugitive slave clause. It said that escaped slaves had to be brought back to their slaveholders. In 1793 Congress passed a Fugitive Slave Act. This act enforced the fugitive slave clause. Anyone caught aiding an escaped slave would be fined.

favor of the proposed amendment. Now it was up to the House.

James Ashley from Ohio had introduced the amendment in December 1863. Ashley was an abolitionist. He wanted slavery to end. He had helped people escape slavery. He hoped the amendment would get enough votes.

The vote was taken. There was not enough support. The amendment fell short by 11 votes.

Ashley would have to bring it back for another vote at a later time. But this vote showed that views on slavery were shifting.

SLAVERY IN THE UNITED STATES

By the 1860s, slavery had been part of the United States for more than 200 years. As the country grew, the Northern and Southern regions developed differently. This led to different political and social views, many of them concerning slavery.

The economy of the South was based on farming. Farmers grew crops such as cotton and tobacco. Large plantation owners depended on enslaved people to work in the fields. Some enslaved people also had duties in the home. They had to clean, cook, and care for their slaveholders' children. They were not paid for the work they did. They worked long hours. Slaveholders could punish their slaves as they saw fit. Punishments included whippings.

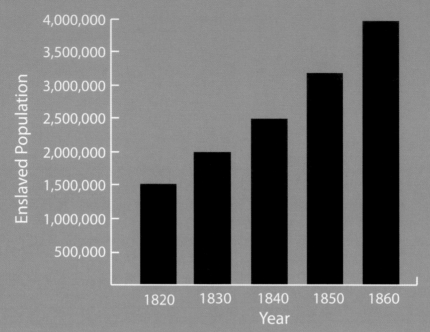

SLAVERY BY THE NUMBERS

The above graph shows the number of enslaved people in the South in the years leading up to the American Civil War (1861–1865). How did the enslaved population in the South change in these years? How does this graph show the South's reliance on slavery?

Slaveholders could sell or buy slaves. Enslaved people were considered property.

Meanwhile, the North became more industrialized. People built factories and businesses. European immigrants came to the North to find work. Many were willing to work for low pay. In these states, slavery was gradually being abolished.

A NEW PRESIDENT

Abraham Lincoln was elected US president in 1860. At that time, nearly 4 million people were enslaved in the South. Lincoln opposed allowing slavery in new states in the West.

After Lincoln's election, many Southerners became more afraid that slavery would be abolished. They feared the federal government would try to end slavery in the South. This tension created a divide. Many people in the South wanted to preserve and

PERSPECTIVES

HARRIET ANN JACOBS

Harriet Ann Jacobs was a former slave. She was born into slavery in North Carolina. She escaped in 1835. She later wrote an autobiography. Her book was called *Incidents in the Life of a Slave Girl*. Jacobs believed it was important to share her story. She wanted to convince people that slavery was wrong.

expand slavery. Many people in the North wanted to end slavery or stop its expansion.

In early 1861, South Carolina left the Union. Soon ten other Southern states followed. They wanted to create a separate country. They called it the Confederate States of America, or the Confederacy. On April 12, 1861, Confederate troops attacked a Union fort. The American Civil War (1861–1865) had begun.

EXPLORE ONLINE
Chapter One discusses some of the issues that led to the Civil War. The article and video on the website below go into more depth on this topic. As you know, every source is different. How is the information from the website the same as the information in Chapter One? What new information did you learn from the website?

HISTORY DETECTIVES: CAUSES OF THE CIVIL WAR
abdocorelibrary.com/thirteenth-amendment

President Abraham Lincoln, *middle*, visited Union troops during the Civil War.

THE EMANCIPATION PROCLAMATION

During the Civil War, Lincoln faced a difficult decision. Lincoln disliked slavery. He did not want slavery to be legal in the new states that entered the Union. But he also did not want to interfere with slavery where it already existed. He thought that each state should have the right to decide whether to abolish slavery. He did not think the federal government should make that decision. He also worried about the border states. These states were located between the Northern and Southern states. They included Delaware,

The Texas African American History Memorial in Austin, Texas, celebrates the day enslaved people were freed in Texas.

Kentucky, Maryland, Missouri, and West Virginia. These were slaveholding states that had remained within the Union. If Lincoln outlawed slavery, they might leave the Union.

A NEW PARTY

There were two major political parties during the Civil War. These parties were called the Republican Party and the Democratic Party. Democrats wanted to preserve slavery. Some Democrats wanted to extend slavery to all the new territories. Others thought each territory's residents should decide for themselves whether to allow slavery. Lincoln was a member of the Republican Party. This was a new party that was founded in 1854. It was created to stop the spread of slavery in the Western territories. The party quickly gained the support of people in the North.

A PRESIDENTIAL ORDER

As the war went on, Lincoln's position began to change. He realized that freeing slaves could help the Union cause. The freed slaves could join the Union forces.

On January 1, 1863, Lincoln issued the Emancipation Proclamation.

Abraham Lincoln, *third from left*, **wrote the Emancipation Proclamation and presented it to his advisers in 1862.**

This was a presidential order. It freed enslaved people in the Confederate states. Lincoln hoped that freed slaves would flee the South and join the Union army. This would weaken the Confederacy and strengthen the Union.

The Emancipation Proclamation did not free all enslaved people. People were still enslaved in the border states and in several Northern states. The Union

FIGHTING FOR UNITY

Frederick Douglass grew up in slavery without his parents. He taught himself to read. He studied speeches about freedom. He escaped slavery when he was 20 years old. He became the most well-known black abolitionist at the time. He gave speeches around the country. In 1863 he gave a speech at a meeting of the American Anti-Slavery Society. He said that the North was fighting for something better than the old Union. The North was fighting for unity. Douglass wanted a country with "no North, no South, no East, no West, no black, no white, but a solidarity of the nation, making every slave free."

army controlled parts of the South. This included parts of Louisiana and Virginia. It also included the state of Tennessee. Enslaved people in these areas were not freed either.

A GUARANTEE OF FREEDOM

The Emancipation Proclamation tied Lincoln to the abolitionists and their cause. Lincoln began to share their view of the war. He started to see the war as the event that would end slavery

COME AND JOIN US BROTHERS.

PUBLISHED BY THE SUPERVISORY COMMITTEE FOR RECRUITING COLORED REGIMENTS
1210 CHESTNUT ST. PHILADELPHIA.

The Union army recruited freed slaves to fight in the war.

in the United States. But the Emancipation Proclamation was an order issued during wartime. The courts could say it was only temporary. They could reverse it after the war ended. Something more was needed to abolish slavery. Abolitionists tried to convince Lincoln that they needed a constitutional amendment.

The African American Civil War Memorial in Washington, DC, honors African Americans who fought in the Civil War.

At first Lincoln thought that the Constitution could not be improved. He believed it should not be changed. But he soon realized that an amendment could help create a stronger country. The United States had been founded on the idea of freedom. Lincoln hoped freedom could become a reality for all Americans.

STRAIGHT TO THE
SOURCE

Although Lincoln opposed slavery, he did not try to abolish it at first. His goal was to save the Union. In 1862 Lincoln wrote a letter to the editor of the *New York Times*. He said:

> *If there be those who would not save the Union unless they could at the same time save Slavery, I do not agree with them. If there be those who would not save the Union unless they could at the same time destroy Slavery, I do not agree with them. My paramount object in this struggle is to save the Union, and is not either to save or destroy Slavery. If I could save the Union without freeing any slave, I would do it, and if I could save it by freeing all the slaves, I would do it, and if I could save it by freeing some and leaving others alone, I would also do that.*

> Source: "A Letter from President Lincoln." *New York Times*. New York Times, August 24, 1862. Web. Accessed July 20, 2018.

Consider Your Audience

Adapt this passage for a different audience, such as a friend. Write a blog post conveying this same information for the new audience. How does your post differ from the original text and why?

THE FIGHT IN CONGRESS

Some congressmen, such as James Ashley, were abolitionists. Ashley was the first representative to call for an amendment that would outlaw slavery. Illinois senator Lyman Trumbull cowrote the amendment. It proposed to free enslaved people. In January 1864, Trumbull's amendment was brought to a committee in the Senate. On February 10, the debate in the Senate began.

Most Democrats were against the amendment. Many said that enslaved people were property. They also argued that the states had rights. These rights included the right

Senator Lyman Trumbull helped write the Thirteenth Amendment.

LYMAN TRUMBULL

Lyman Trumbull was a lawyer and a senator. He helped write the Thirteenth Amendment. He also wrote the Freedmen's Bureau Act of 1865. This act created a federal agency called the Bureau of Refugees, Freedmen, and Abandoned Lands. This agency was commonly called the Freedmen's Bureau. It helped African Americans in their transition from slavery to freedom. It trained African Americans to become teachers. It built hospitals and schools for African Americans. Trumbull later wrote the Civil Rights Act of 1866. This act helped protect the rights of African Americans.

to keep or abolish slavery. Republicans argued in favor of the amendment. They believed that enslaved people should be freed.

On April 8, the Senate passed the amendment by a vote of 38 to 6. On June 15, the House of Representatives voted on the amendment. The amendment did not pass. The abolitionists would have to try again.

THE FINAL VOTE

In 1864 Lincoln was up for reelection. He won the election by a landslide. The Republicans gained more members in Congress. Abolitionists believed these events came about from the public's desire to end slavery. They put more pressure on the representatives to pass the amendment.

On January 31, 1865, the House of Representatives voted again on the amendment. The room where the vote took place was packed with spectators. They included Supreme Court justices and free African Americans. The amendment passed. The crowd erupted in cheers.

Lincoln signed the amendment to show his approval. The amendment was then sent to each of the states to be ratified. An amendment has to be approved by three-fourths of the states. At the time, 36 states were in the Union or in rebellion in the South. That meant 27 states had to ratify the amendment.

Illinois ratified the amendment on February 1, 1865. It was the first state to approve the amendment. By the end of the month, a total of 18 states had approved it. The support of nine more states was needed for the amendment to become part of the Constitution.

The Civil War came to an end as the amendment was being considered by the states. In April 1865, Confederate general Robert E. Lee's troops surrendered. The North won the war. The Union was saved.

MORE PROBLEMS

On December 6, 1865, Georgia became the twenty-seventh state to ratify the Thirteenth Amendment. Three-fourths of the states had approved the amendment. It became part of the Constitution. Eventually all of the states would ratify the amendment. The last state to endorse it was Mississippi.

The Lincoln Memorial in Washington, DC, honors Abraham Lincoln's legacy.

THOMAS D. ELIOT

Thomas D. Eliot was a US representative for the state of Massachusetts. He was an abolitionist. He wanted African Americans to have the same rights as white people. In 1866 Eliot made a speech to Congress. He described slavery as "the knot which politicians could not untie during eighty years of peace." He praised Lincoln for ending slavery. But he said freeing enslaved people was not enough. It was now the government's job to protect the freed slaves. He argued that the government should pass laws to protect the rights of African Americans.

Mississippi did not officially ratify the amendment until 2013.

Lincoln had hoped the Thirteenth Amendment would end the problems caused by slavery. It did not have this effect. The amendment freed enslaved people. But there were many problems it did not fix.

STRAIGHT TO THE
SOURCE

Noah Brooks was a newspaper reporter. He was in the room when the House of Representatives approved the Thirteenth Amendment. He described the crowd's reaction:

> *For a moment there was a pause of utter silence, as if the voices of the dense mass of spectators were choked by strong emotion. Then there was an explosion, a storm of cheers, the like of which probably no Congress of the United States ever heard before. Strong men embraced each other with tears. The galleries and aisles were bristling with standing, cheering crowds. The air was stirred with a cloud of women's handkerchiefs waving and floating; hands were shaking; men threw their arms about each other's necks. . . .*
>
> *The air was rent by the thunder of a great salute fired on Capitol Hill, to notify all who heard that slavery was no more.*
>
> Source: Noah Brooks. *Washington in Lincoln's Time*. New York: The Century Company, 1896. Print. 207.

What's the Big Idea?
Take a close look at this passage. What does Brooks's description tell you about the spectators in the room? How does this description reveal a change in Americans' attitudes about slavery?

FOUR

THE LOOPHOLE

After the Thirteenth Amendment passed, the South lost its enslaved workers. Enslaved people had provided free labor. Slavery boosted the Southern economy. But there was a loophole in the amendment. The amendment outlawed slavery except as a form of punishment. People who were convicted of a crime could be forced to work. Law enforcement officers began arresting black men at a high rate. The men were often convicted of minor crimes such as theft.

In 1865 and 1866, Southern lawmakers created new laws. These laws were called black codes. It was a crime for a black person

In the late 1800s and early 1900s, many black prisoners were chained together and forced to do manual labor. Some prisoners were children.

THE BLACK CODES

Slavery allowed white people to control black people. White people looked for new ways to control black people after slavery ended. The black codes allowed Southerners to do this. Historian Khalil Muhammad explains, "White Southerners were absolutely horrified . . . that people they had once owned were now their equals. The plain and simple fact was that for them, the world had literally been turned upside down. And in every way possible, they attempted to turn that world right-side up again."

to be unemployed and homeless. The punishment was prison, fines, or forced labor. Some black men were arrested just for speaking to white women.

The South created a system called convict leasing. Black prisoners were sold to companies who bid the most money. The companies forced them to do hard labor. This labor included working in mines and building railroads. Prisoners were not paid for their work. In these ways, slavery was reconstructed through the prison system.

VIOLENCE IN THE SOUTH

After slavery ended, free black people formed towns in the South. Some registered to vote. Some ran for political office. Others started their own businesses. Many white people did not like the fact that black people had these new freedoms. Some white people formed a group called the Ku Klux Klan (KKK). The KKK and other white people would gather in mobs and lynch black people. They killed thousands across the country. They usually hanged black people from trees. These lynchings were often thought of as a punishment for a crime. But there did not have to be proof that a crime happened. A rumor that a black person had committed a crime was enough.

JIM CROW LAWS

In the 1870s, Southern states created Jim Crow laws. These laws enforced racial segregation. Racial segregation is the separation of people into groups based on their races. Jim Crow laws separated white and black people. Black people had to use different services and facilities, such as bathrooms. Fear of crime was at the root of segregation laws. White people were told that they needed protection from black people. They thought the only way to achieve this was through segregation.

Jim Crow laws were enforced for more than 50 years. Opposition to these laws finally led to their downfall. The American civil rights movement grew in

THE BIRTH OF A NATION

In 1915 a film called *The Birth of a Nation* was released. The film was about the Civil War. It told the story through the South's perspective. In the film, black Union troops take over a Southern city. KKK members save white people in the city. The film depicted black people as criminals. Members of the KKK were depicted as the heroes. Black actors were not even cast in the film. White actors wore black makeup on their faces. They pretended to be African Americans. White people who saw this film associated black people with crime.

the 1950s and 1960s. Black people demanded fair and equal treatment.

The Civil Rights Act was passed in 1964. It ended segregation. It banned employment discrimination. People could not be denied a job because of their race. The Voting Rights Act was passed in 1965. It outlawed obstacles that had kept black people from voting. Many black people were hopeful. They saw these acts as a turning point. But black people were still discriminated against in other ways. Black men continued to be jailed at high rates. The Thirteenth Amendment's loophole had created this problem.

FURTHER EVIDENCE

Chapter Four discusses the black codes. What was one of the main points of this chapter? What evidence is included to support this point? Read the article at the website below. Does the information on the website support this point? Does it present new evidence?

BLACK CODES AND PIG LAWS
abdocorelibrary.com/thirteenth-amendment

THE WAR ON CRIME

In 1968 Richard Nixon was elected president of the United States. He declared a war on crime. He wanted to bring down the crime rate. His main focus was drug-related crimes. Many people associated these crimes with black people. Police arrested many African Americans. Black people were not more likely to use or sell drugs than white people. But they were nearly three times as likely to be arrested for drug use.

MANDATORY SENTENCES

Later presidents continued to target black people in the war on crime. Ronald Reagan

Today black people continue to be imprisoned at a higher rate than white people.

became president in 1980. He increased mandatory sentences for drug crimes. A mandatory sentence is the minimum amount of time someone is required to be imprisoned for a crime. Crack cocaine users were given a longer mandatory sentence than powder cocaine users. Black populations were more likely to use crack cocaine than powder cocaine. White people more often used powder cocaine. Some people argued that crack cocaine users received harsher sentences because they were more likely to be African American.

WILLIE HORTON

Willie Horton was a black inmate at a Massachusetts prison in 1987. On a weekend leave from prison, Horton raped a woman and beat her boyfriend. George H. W. Bush was a presidential candidate in 1988. He used Horton's story to raise fears about crime. He said that criminals do not deserve weekends off. Bush did not mention race. But Horton's photo was everywhere. People linked violence with African Americans. They demanded harsher punishments for criminals.

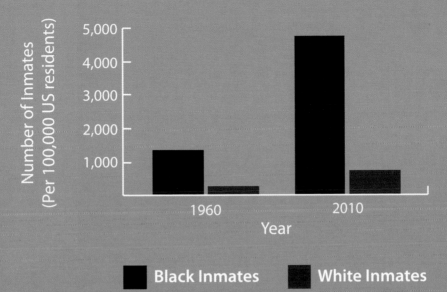

INCARCERATION RATES

Black Inmates **White Inmates**

The above graph compares the rate of black and white incarceration in the United States in 1960 and 2010. What differences do you notice? How do you think these incarceration rates may change in the future?

MASS IMPRISONMENT

The United States has just 4 percent of the world's population. But it holds approximately 22 percent of the world's prison population. Activists say the US prison system needs to be changed. African Americans make up approximately 40 percent of the US prison population.

Some experts say the US economy relies on prison labor. Inmates who are physically able to work are required to do so. Some inmates answer customer service calls. Others work on farms. Inmates are usually not paid much. For example, Louisiana pays its inmates just four cents per hour. In some state-run prisons, inmates are not paid for certain jobs. Some people say this labor system is a type of modern-day slavery.

The Thirteenth Amendment's loophole led to the mass imprisonment

THREE-STRIKES LAW

In 1994 President Bill Clinton passed the Violent Crime Control and Law Enforcement Act. Part of the act included harsher punishments for criminals. One of those punishments was called the three-strikes law. This law said that anyone who had two or more previous convictions, at least one of which was a violent felony, would get life in prison as punishment for their third conviction. Opponents of the law say it hurt black people more than white people. Today some lawmakers are trying to reduce the three-strikes punishment to 25 years in prison.

of African Americans. The public associated black people with crime. This stereotype persists today. Police continue to arrest black people at a higher rate than white people. In 2016 the documentary *13th* was released. Filmmaker Ava DuVernay explores the link between the Thirteenth Amendment's loophole and mass incarceration. DuVernay and other activists are working to shed light on the injustices of the US prison system.

PERSPECTIVES

ANGELA DAVIS

Angela Davis is a distinguished professor at the University of California, Santa Cruz. She was unfairly arrested in 1970. This experience motivated her to speak out against the prison system. She protested to improve prison conditions. Today Davis remains a civil rights activist. She protests police violence against black people. She says, "There is an unbroken line of police violence in the United States that takes us all the way back to the days of slavery, the aftermath of slavery, [and] the development of the Ku Klux Klan."

FAST FACTS

- Abraham Lincoln was elected president of the United States in 1860. Soon after Lincoln's election, 11 Southern states left the Union. They formed the Confederacy. The Confederacy wanted to allow slavery. But many people in the Union wanted to abolish it. This disagreement led to the Civil War.

- Lincoln issued the Emancipation Proclamation in 1863. This order freed enslaved people who lived in the Confederate states.

- In January 1865, the House of Representatives approved the Thirteenth Amendment. The amendment became part of the US Constitution in December 1865. It freed all people.

- The Thirteenth Amendment outlawed slavery except as a form of punishment. Police began arresting black people in large numbers. Black prisoners were forced to work. This created a type of modern-day slavery.

- In the mid-1900s, politicians wanted to control crime rates and drug abuse. They created harsher punishments for drug possession. They often targeted black people. Black people were arrested at a higher rate than white people.

- Today black people continue to be arrested in large numbers. Activists are attempting to change the prison system.

STOP AND
THINK

Dig Deeper

After reading this book, what questions do you still have about the Thirteenth Amendment and its legacy? With an adult's help, find a few reliable sources that can help you answer your questions. Write a paragraph about what you learned.

Why Do I Care?

The Thirteenth Amendment was ratified more than 150 years ago. How do you think its legacy affects people in the United States today? How might your life or your friends' lives be different if the Thirteenth Amendment had not been passed?

You Are There

Chapter Three discusses the debate in the US Congress over the Thirteenth Amendment. Imagine you were in the House of Representatives when the amendment finally passed. Write a letter home telling your family what happened. Be sure to add plenty of details.

GLOSSARY

abolish
to officially end or do away with something

abolitionist
someone who was against slavery

conviction
a court ruling that finds a person guilty

discrimination
the unjust treatment of a person or group based on race or other perceived differences

felony
a serious crime, such as robbery or murder

immigrant
a person who leaves one country to live in another country

industrialize
to develop factories and businesses in an area

plantation
a large farm where workers grow crops

ratify
to give legal or official approval of something

segregation
the separation of people of different races or ethnic groups through separate schools and other public spaces

stereotype
a common belief about a group of people that is usually negative and untrue

ONLINE
RESOURCES

To learn more about the Thirteenth Amendment and its legacy, visit our free resource websites below.

Visit **abdocorelibrary.com** or scan this QR code for free Common Core resources for teachers and students, including vetted activities, multimedia, and booklinks, for deeper subject comprehension.

Visit **abdobooklinks.com** or scan this QR code for free additional online weblinks for further learning. These links are routinely monitored and updated to provide the most current information available.

LEARN
MORE

Kneib, Martha. *The Civil War through the Eyes of Abraham Lincoln*. Minneapolis, MN: Abdo Publishing, 2016.

Winter, Max. *The Civil Rights Movement*. Minneapolis, MN: Abdo Publishing, 2015.

ABOUT THE
AUTHORS

Duchess Harris, JD, PhD

Dr. Harris is a professor of American Studies at Macalester College and curator of the Duchess Harris Collection of ABDO books. She is also the coauthor of the titles in the collection, which features popular selections such as *Hidden Human Computers: The Black Women of NASA* and series including News Literacy and Being Female in America.

Before working with ABDO, Dr. Harris authored several other books on the topics of race, culture, and American history. She served as an associate editor for *Litigation News*, the American Bar Association Section of Litigation's quarterly flagship publication, and was the first editor in chief of *Law Raza*, an interactive online journal covering race and the law, published at William Mitchell College of Law. She has earned a PhD in American Studies from the University of Minnesota and a JD from William Mitchell College of Law.

Samantha S. Bell

Samantha S. Bell lives with her family in upstate South Carolina. She graduated from Furman University with a degree in history and a teaching certification in social studies. She is the author of more than 90 nonfiction books for children.

INDEX